Shari Frey   July 1996

PEARLS
for
PARENTS

—

A Wealth of Wisdom on Raising Children

Compiled by
JOYCE VOLLMER BROWN

The C.R. Gibson Company
Norwalk, Connecticut

*In memory of a dear father who taught by quiet example;
with gratitude for the most wonderful mother
I could ever hope to have.*

Published by The C.R. Gibson Company, Norwalk, CT 06856
ISBN 0-8378-9860-9
GB729
Book design by Susan Hood

Scripture verses marked (TLB) are taken from The Living Bible, copyright 1971. Used
by permission of Tyndale House Publishers, Inc., Wheaton, IL 60189. All rights
reserved. Scripture marked (RSV) are from the Revised Standard Version of the Bible,
copyright 1946, 1952, 1971, 1973, Division of Christian Education, National Council
of the Churches of Christ in the USA. All rights reserved. Scripture quotations marked
(NIV) are taken from the Holy Bible, New International Version(R). NIV(R). Copyright
1973, 1978, 1984 by International Bible Society. Used by permission of Zondervan
Publishing House. All rights reserved. Scripture marked (KJV) is from the
King James Version of the Bible.

The acknowledgments that appear in the back of this book hereby constitute an exten-
sion of this copyright page.

Contents

Introduction

As parents, we influence our children in many ways. . . how they feel about themselves, look at life, get along with others and perceive God. Every decision we make and action we take affects them directly or indirectly. Every day we have the opportunity to mold their lives and help them down the right path.

Fulfilling this awesome responsibility is a tremendous challenge. We want the very best for our children, but we doubt we possess enough wisdom, patience and strength to give it to them.

In previous times society supported parents' efforts to raise children with strong moral values. But today's world seems to bombard children with messages contradicting what parents are trying to teach. Questionable role models, their own peers, and the media often advocate empty, self-centered, undesirable lifestyles.

It is harder than ever to teach children to stand firm to Biblical principles, to stand out from the crowd, and ultimately to make a difference in their world. With God's help, we can teach them to live in ways pleasing to Him.

This treasury is one to refer to whenever you feel discouraged, frustrated or anxious in bringing up your children. It is my hope that these quotations from great men and women of the past, God's Word, and contemporary Christian leaders will provide practical advice and reassuring encouragement along the way.

Joyce Vollmer Brown

Accepting Our Children

Children arrive in our arms longing to be known, longing to accept themselves as they are, to be who they are. So when they wade into the swift current of their times, they will be able to stand firm, and won't depend on peer pressure to give them their standard. They won't need to be accepted by the group nearly as much.

Charles R. Swindoll

And as we accept our children, we free them to be who they are in a world that is trying to tell them every day to be someone else.

Tim Hansel

Accept one another, then just as Christ accepted you, in order to bring praise to God.

Romans 15:7, NIV

God knows us totally, and yet accepts us completely. That's the pattern: His acceptance of you is the model of your acceptance of your child.

Howard G. Hendricks

Love makes everything lovely.

George MacDonald

Once the realization is accepted that even between the closest human beings infinite distances continue to exist, a wonderful living side by side can grow up, if they succeed in loving the distance between them which makes it possible for each to see the other whole against the sky.

Rainer Maria Rilke

I am convinced that as we begin to feel comfortable in our own identity, we stop trying to make other people conform to what we think they should be.

Bruce Larson

Love between persons means that each wants the other to be more himself.

M. C. D'Arcy, S. J.

If I were asked what single qualification was necessary for one who has the care of children, I should say patience—patience with their tempers, with their understandings, with their progress.

Francois de S. Fenelon

By the very nature of our position as parents, we are inclined to over-push. We pour our little ones into molds of our making. . . We drive. We coerce. We bribe. We threaten. We live our broken dreams again as we hurry them toward the future. We compare our product with neighbors, classmates, brothers, sisters, cousins, the boss's child. We measure by "What will people think?"

Charlie Shedd

When was the last time you told your children that you accept them unconditionally, no matter how they do in class, on the athletic field, or in the school orchestra?

Tim Hansel

All true love is founded on esteem.

George Villiers Buckingham

Are you on your child's back or on his team? Get off his back; get on his team.

Howard G. Hendricks

* Acceptance means respecting a child's feelings and his personality while letting him know that wrong behavior is unacceptable. Acceptance means that parents like the child all the time, regardless of his acts or ideas.

John M. Drescher

We can give our kids increasing amounts of assurance and esteem. We can send them messages many times a day that say, "You are okay."

Tim Hansel

* Why is it important to affirm a child? Because a child who is truly accepted by his parents. . . can grow up learning to accept himself. . . He'll be able to admit his own failures and weaknesses. He'll be able to forget about himself and love others.

Anne Ortlund

When a child lives with parents who believe in him, he instinctively holds a higher view of himself and his brothers and sisters as well. Everybody's sense of worth is enhanced.

Howard G. Hendricks

Overcoming Anger

The most common error in disciplining children, and perhaps the most costly, is the *inappropriate use of anger* in attempting to control boys and girls. There is no more ineffective method of leading human beings (of all ages) than the use of irritation and anger.

Dr. James Dobson

Yelling and nagging at children can become a habit, and an ineffectual one at that!. . . Parents often use anger to get action, instead of using action to get action. It doesn't work.

Dr. James Dobson

Rebuke not in anger, or with severity; hard words are like hailstones in summer, beating down and destroying what they would nourish were they melted into drops.

Unknown

A torn jacket is soon mended; but hard words bruise the heart of a child.

Henry Wadsworth Longfellow

Whoso keepeth his mouth and his tongue keepeth his soul from troubles.

Proverbs 21:23, KJV

Be not rash with thy mouth.

Ecclesiastes 5:2, KJV

And the Lord's servant must not quarrel; instead, he must be kind to everyone, able to teach, not resentful.

II Timothy 2:24, NIV

For man's anger does not bring about the righteous life that God desires.

James 1:20, NIV

He that is soon angry dealeth foolishly.

Proverbs 14:17, KJV

The greatest remedy for anger is delay.

Seneca

Be not hasty in thy spirit to be angry; for anger resteth in the bosom of fools.

Ecclesiastes 7:9, KJV

Another thing that seems to improve the longer you keep it is your temper.

Unknown

Cease from anger, and forsake wrath: fret not thyself in any wise to do evil.

Psalms 37:8, KJV

He who can suppress a moment's anger may prevent a day of sorrow.

Unknown

When angry, count ten before you speak; if very angry, count a hundred.
Thomas Jefferson

Be ever gentle with the children God has given you. Watch over them constantly; reprove them earnestly, but not in anger. "Yes, they are good boys," said a kind father. "I talk to them much, but I do not beat my children: the world will beat them." It was a beautiful thought, though not elegantly expressed.

Elihu Burritt

Don't be a lion in your own house.

Czech Proverb

Anger, even when it punishes the faults of delinquents, ought not to precede reason as its mistress, but attend as a handmaid at the back of reason, to come to the front when bidden. For once it begins to take control of the mind, it calls just what it does cruelly.

St. Gregory the Great

It's been said that Gandhi had this sign on a wall in his home: "When you are in the right you can afford to keep your temper, and when you are in the wrong, you cannot afford to lose it."

Any time a child involves us in a power struggle he has won control. . . Whenever a child makes us lose our temper, he has won a victory. . . The first hint of a power struggle is our attitude. Whenever we feel angry or frustrated, we are in a power struggle no matter what we do! Children read us like an open book.

Dr. Bruce Narramore

Anyone who angers you conquers you.

Unknown

A man should study ever to keep cool. He makes his inferiors his superiors by heat.

Ralph Waldo Emerson

Am I acting or reacting? Am I losing my temper because he lost his?. . . Good question: Will I go down to his level or bring him up to mine?

Charlie Shedd

An angry man stirs up dissension, and a hot-tempered one commits many sins.

Proverbs 29:22, NIV

How much more grievous are the consequences of anger than the causes of it!

Marcus Aurelius

Consider how much more you often suffer from your anger and grief, than from those very things for which you are angry and grieved.

Marcus Antonius

To be angry is to revenge the faults of others upon ourselves.

Alexander Pope

He that hath no rule over his own spirit is like a city that is broken down, and without walls.

Proverbs 25:28, KJV

Anger would inflict punishment on another; meanwhile, it tortures itself.

Publilius Syrus

When tempers grow hot, Christianity grows cold.
Unknown

If you lose your head, how do you expect to be able to use it?

Unknown

A man in a passion rides a mad horse.

Benjamin Franklin

"There's nothing wrong with losing my temper," a lady once told evangelist Billy Sunday, "I blow up, and then it's over with."

"So does a shotgun," the evangelist replied, "but look at the damage left behind."

Little secret for big help—in angry moments, lower your volume. A soft answer may disarm your antagonist. It takes him by surprise.

Charlie Shedd

A soft answer turns away wrath, but a harsh word stirs up anger.

Proverbs 15:1, RSV

The next time you get angry with your children, try thinking of them as precious antique vases. How likely would you be to pick up a priceless vase in your living room and shake it around? The value you attach to it would make you check your behavior. The same thing should be true of your living treasures.

*Gary Smalley and
John Trent, Ph.D.*

We have very little direct control over our emotions but we have maximum control over our behavior.

Charles R. Swindoll

Let not anyone say that he cannot govern his passions, nor hinder them from breaking out and carrying him into action; for what he can do before a prince or a great man, he can do alone, or in the presence of God if he will.

John Locke

Instilling Christian Values

In a race, the one who carries the baton and hands it to someone else takes a big risk. . . If we don't hand over the baton to our children—the values God gave us and the principles of faith we live by—it doesn't matter how fast they can run.

Mary C. Crowley

Train up a child in the way he should go: and when he is old, he will not depart from it.

Proverbs 22:6, KJV

Inculcating Christian standards is like building a fire in the rain. It requires willful determination, against all odds, to do what seems impossible. It calls for expertise—know-how which understands the stubborn nature of the child and the nature of a hostile world. It demands a stubborn perseverance to keep fanning the flickering flame, to keep protecting the hot coals.

Howard G. Hendricks

Just as the twig is bent, the tree is inclined.

Alexander Pope

Morals are an acquirement—like music, like a foreign language, like piety. . . no man is born with them.

Mark Twain

Knowledge does not comprise all which is contained in the large term of education. The feelings are to be disciplined; the passions are to be restrained; true and worthy motives are to be inspired; a profound religious feeling is to be instilled, and pure morality inculcated under all circumstances. All this is comprised in education.

Daniel Webster

They who provide much wealth for their children but neglect to improve them in virtue, do like those who feed their horses high, but never train them to be useful.

Socrates

Educate men without religion and you make of them but clever devils.

Duke of Wellington

If you fail to inculcate in your children the moral standards that you want them to have, they are going to adopt the moral standards that are taught to them by their peers and by the television and music industries.

Patrick J. Jeske

America's future will be determined by the home and school. The child becomes largely what it is taught, hence we must watch what we teach it, and how we live before it.

Jane Addams

The bulwark of religious training is vital if the line is to be held against the forces of corruption, crime and disloyalty. I believe that men imbued with spiritual values do not betray their country. I believe that children reared in homes in which morality is taught and lived rarely become delinquents.

J. Edgar Hoover

All thy children shall be taught of the Lord; and great shall be the peace of thy children.

Isaiah 54:13, KJV

Teach them the good way wherein they should walk.

I Kings 8:36, KJV

The conscience of children is formed by the influences that surround them; their notions of good and evil are the result of the moral atmosphere they breathe.

Jean Paul Richter

A person's conscience is largely a gift from his parents—from their training and instruction and approval and disapproval. The way right and wrong are taught throughout the first decade of life will never be completely forgotten—even though it may be contradicted later.

Dr. James Dobson

Our responsibility as parents is to develop in our children a hunger, taste, or desire for spiritual things. This is not the picture of "you do as I say," but a process of cultivating the personal urge to love God and follow Him.

David Jeremiah

Let the word of Christ dwell in you richly in all wisdom; teaching and admonishing one another in psalms and hymns and spiritual songs, singing with grace in your hearts to the Lord.

Colossians 3:16, KJV

And let us consider how we may spur one another on toward love and good deeds.

Hebrews 10:24, NIV

During any given week there are dozens of opportunities to communicate God's way. And it's all so natural, so real. . . Questions and conflicts come to the surface which provide a marvelous base for training. Wise is the parent who stays alert and capitalizes on such opportunities.

Charles R. Swindoll

Exhort one another daily, while it is called Today; lest any of you be hardened through the deceitfulness of sin.

Hebrews 3:13, KJV

Precept must be upon precept, precept upon precept; line upon line, line upon line; here a little, and there a little.

Isaiah 28:10, KJV

These commandments that I give you today are to be upon your hearts. Impress them on your children. Talk about them when you sit at home and when you walk along the road, when you lie down and when you get up.

Deuteronomy 6:6-7, NIV

All Scripture is God-breathed and is useful for teaching, rebuking, correcting and training in righteousness, so that the man of God may be thoroughly equipped for every good work.

II Timothy 3:16-17, NIV

It is our job to convince our children the consequences of sin are far worse than temporary pleasures which may come.

Charles R. Swindoll

It helps to talk about an issue ahead of time. If you want them to think through whether or not they will ever drink, begin at an age when it isn't a problem. If the issue is whether or not they will have premarital sex, discuss it before they become emotionally involved with someone.

Jim and Sally Conway

One of the questions I ask parents is, "Are you raising a giver or a taker?" With all this tendency to push kids to grow up too fast, they learn to be far better at acquiring, collecting, and achieving for

themselves than they are at serving, sharing, and giving to others.

Dr. Kevin Leman

"Practice staging everyday situations with your children," a minister once told me, "and role play the ways a person can say no to something he doesn't want to do."

Denise Turner

Even a child is known by his doings, whether his work be pure, and whether it be right.

Proverbs 20:11, KJV

One mother has always let her children help her bake cakes for the bereaved and go along on visits to church shut-ins. "You can't expect children to believe you care about people if they never see you do anything for anyone," she explained.

Denise Turner

Communicating Effectively

Some so speak in exaggerations and superlatives that we need to make a large discount from their statements before we can come at their real meaning.

Tryon Edwards

The most influential of all educational factors is the conversation in a child's home.

William Temple

A word spoken in due season, how good is it!

Proverbs 15:23, KJV

In communicating with children, perhaps the most serious mistake parents make is the volume they use.

Zig Ziglar

Other forms of discipline are largely corrective. They are "after the fact." But communication is a great preventative. When parents and children have mutual self-respect and are communicating well, many misbehaviors are avoided.

Dr. Bruce Narramore

Nothing lowers the level of conversation more than raising the voice.

Unknown

Save yelling only for the "biggies." The more you yell, the less they'll listen.

Freda Ingle Briggs

The only people who really listen to an argument are the neighbors.

Unknown

He who establishes his argument by noise and command, shows that his reason is weak.

Michel E. de Montaigne

Speak to the child in the same tone of voice you would use with your best friend.

Margaret F. Skutch

Isn't there a better way to raise a child than raising our voices? Isn't there an alternative to giving lecture #202 which the kids have memorized? They even correct you if you skip part of it.

Gary Smalley and John Trent, Ph.D.

Talk low, talk slow, and don't say too much.

John Wayne

Kind words cost no more than unkind ones. Kind words produce kind actions, not only on the part of those to whom they are addressed, but on the part of those by whom they are employed.

Jeremy Bentham

When you introduce a moral lesson let it be brief.

Horace

Avoid nagging. I often recall Ann Landers' description which I read several years ago: Nagging is like being nibbled to death by a duck.

Joyce Vollmer Brown

But I tell you that men will have to give account on the day of judgment for every careless word they have spoken.

Matthew 12:36, NIV

Have something to say; say it, and stop when you've done.

Tryon Edwards

Be humble and gentle in your conversation; and of few words, I charge you; but always pertinent when you speak.

William Penn

In many a Christian home a child is told what he may and may not do—but is not trained to understand why. That method, quite frankly, is lethal. . . Deep within, he lacks the rationale, the conviction necessary to stand alone against a powerful world system.

Charles R. Swindoll

Let your speech be always with grace, seasoned with salt, that ye may know how ye ought to answer every man.

Colossians 4:6, KJV

We are told the average child asks 500,000 questions by the age of fifteen. That's half a million opportunities to teach. Many of these are "why" and "how" questions which take us right to the feet of God.

John M. Drescher

A man finds joy in giving an apt reply—and how good is a timely word.

Proverbs 15:23, NIV

One important key to communication on any issue or subject is to end every conversation with a comma, not a period.

Zig Ziglar

If you look directly into children's eyes, they are much more likely to concentrate on what you are saying and remember it than if you were to look elsewhere.

Margaret F. Skutch

Encourage your children to give you feedback so that you know you're getting through.

Tim Hansel

If you have trouble getting (your child) to talk, try talking to her at bedtime. She will be willing to discuss anything in order to postpone going to sleep.

Denise Turner

Words are such a powerful tool. They can encourage or discourage, accept or deny, create hope or depression. Are you realizing the power of words in your own home? How much time do you actually spend talking with (not to) your kids each week?

Tim Hansel

Kids may forget what you said. . . but they'll never forget how you made them feel.

Carl W. Buehner

Disciplining with Love

Discipline involves the total molding of the child's character through encouraging good behavior and correcting unacceptable behavior. Punishment is the part of discipline which provides a short-term, temporary deterrent.

John M. Drescher

Discipline can take many forms—denial of privileges, holding back the use of a special possession, or isolation for a short period of time—but praise and rewards for a job well done is often the most effective approach for training our children and building healthy self-esteem.

David Jeremiah

Correction does much, but encouragement does more.—Encouragement after censure is as the sun after a shower.

Johann Wolfgang von Goethe

To discipline a child is not to punish him for stepping out of line, but to teach that child the way he ought to go. Discipline therefore includes everything that you do in order to help children learn.

Henry R. Brandt

If ever a child needs the tenderness and presence of a parent, it is after the administration of discipline.

Charles R. Swindoll

The effectiveness of corrective discipline is always determined by the relationship you build in preventive discipline. For example, I ask, "Do you play with your child?" If you don't play with him, you have no right to spank him.

Howard G. Hendricks

We must truly serve those whom we appear to command; we must bear with their imperfections, correct them with gentleness and patience, and lead them in the way to heaven.

Francis de S. Fenelon

Nothing is so strong as gentleness; nothing so gentle as real strength.

Francis de Sales

The key to interacting effectively with your children is to think before you discipline.

Dr. Kevin Leman

When children misbehave, we usually need to start the disciplinary measures by discussion rather than by the use of parental power.

Dr. Bruce Narramore

And now a word to you parents. Don't keep on scolding and nagging your children, making them angry and resentful. Rather, bring them up with the loving discipline the Lord himself approves, with suggestions and godly advice.

Ephesians 6:4, TLB

Soft-hearted mothers rear soft-hearted children. They hurt them for life because they are afraid of hurting them when they are young. Coddle your children and they will turn out noodles. . . Children without chastisement are fields without plowing.

Charles Spurgeon

No discipline seems pleasant at the time, but painful. Later on, however, it produces a harvest of righteousness and peace for those who have been trained by it.

Hebrews 12:11, NIV

With children we must mix gentleness with firmness. They must not always have their own way, but they must not always be thwarted. If we never have headaches through rebuking them, we shall have plenty of heartaches as they grow up. Be obeyed at all costs; for if you yield up your authority once, you will hardly get it again.

Charles Haddon Spurgeon

Chasten thy son while there is hope. . .

Proverbs 19:18, KJV

Correct thy son, and he shall give thee rest; yea, he shall give delight unto thy soul.

Proverbs 29:17, KJV

Discipline and order are part of the natural laws of the universe. The child who has not been disciplined with love

by his little world (the family) will be disciplined, generally without love, by the big world.

Zig Ziglar

If you refuse to discipline your son, it proves you don't love him; for if you love him you will be prompt to punish him.

Proverbs 13:24, TLB

Every great person first learned how to obey, whom to obey, and when to obey.

Unknown

Appropriate punishment is not something parents do to a beloved child; it is something done for him or her.

Dr. James Dobson

They have a right to censure that have a heart to help.

William Penn

Children cannot be made good by making them happy, but they can be made happy by making them good.

E. J. Kiefer

Children have strong feelings and impulsive wishes. While they seek to extend their boundaries and reach their unknown limits, they also become anxious and insecure when no limits are available.

Dr. Bruce Narramore

How then, are we to shape the will while preserving the spirit intact? It is accomplished by establishing reasonable boundaries and enforcing them with love, but by avoiding any implication that the child is unwanted, unnecessary, foolish, ugly, dumb, a burden, an embarrassment, or a disastrous mistake.

Dr. James Dobson

Provoke not your children to anger, lest they be discouraged.

Colossians 3:21, KJV

Fair discipline administered out of love builds self-esteem and will elicit a positive response. Arbitrary discipline, based on sheer power, tears down the child and provides reaction.

Paul Lewis

If parents carry (discipline) lovingly towards their children, mixing their mercies with loving rebukes, and their loving rebukes with fatherly and motherly compassions, they are more likely to save their children than being churlish and severe towards them.

John Bunyan

We will want our children. . . to fear the consequences of certain actions rather than fearing us. In an orderly and objective way we can point out to a child that life is a series of choices and that certain choices bring about certain results.

Alan Loy McGinnis

Consistency is perhaps the most important ingredient in proper discipline. . . Something that was wrong yesterday is wrong today. Something that brought the rod last week should bring the rod this week.

Charles R. Swindoll

When I discipline my children, I want them to feel bad about their misbehavior, but good about themselves.

Spencer Johnson, M.D.

Enjoying Life Together

Yes, *someday* when the kids are grown, things are going to be a lot different. . . The house will be quiet. . . and calm. . . and always clean. . . and empty. . . and filled with memories. . . and lonely. . . and we won't like that at all. And we'll spend our time not looking forward to *Someday* but looking back to *Yesterday*. And thinking, "Maybe we can baby-sit the grandkids and get some *life* back in this place for a change!"

Charles R. Swindoll

We need to learn to enjoy our children more. Maybe not when the dog has forgotten to scratch on the door and the soup is boiling over on the stove and everyone in the house is fighting to watch favorite TV shows—but we ought to enjoy our children sometimes. Perhaps even most of the time.

Denise Turner

What we have, we prize, not to the worth while we enjoy it; but being lacked and lost, why then we rack the value; then we find the virtue that possession would not show us while it was ours.

William Shakespeare

Putting the present in the past makes me understand how wonderful it is to be at this stage right now with my children.

Freda Ingle Briggs

Parents in the twentieth century have saddled themselves with unnecessary guilt, fear and self-doubt. That is not the divine plan. Throughout the Scriptures, it is quite clear that the raising of children was viewed as a wonderful blessing from God—a welcome, joyful experience.

Dr. James Dobson

Lo, children are an heritage of the Lord: and the fruit of the womb is his reward. As arrows are in the hand of a mighty man; so are children of the youth. Happy is the man that hath his quiver full of them.

Psalms 127:3-5, KJV

I have a friend who has always been really good at having fun with her kids. "You wanted children, didn't you?" she often says to people. "Then play with them. Have fun with them."

Denise Turner

Happy is he that is happy in his children.

Thomas Fuller

Our home joys are the most delightful earth affords, and the joy of parents in their children is the most holy joy of humanity. It makes their hearts pure and good, it lifts men up to their Father in heaven.

Johann Heinrich Pestalozzi

A happy family is but an earlier heaven.

John Bowring

Laughter is the key to survival during the special stresses of the child-rearing years. If you can see the delightful side of your assignment, you can also deal with the difficult.

Dr. James Dobson

Laughter is healthy, no doubt about it. Think about your verbal reactions to your children. Are you doing more yelling—or more laughing? Which creates the least amount of stress?

Freda Ingle Briggs

Parents earn the attention of their children for serious matters by showing their love for the light-hearted.

Dean and Grace Merrill

Give me a sense of humor, Lord;
Give me the grace to see a joke,
To get some happiness from life;
And pass it on to other folk.

Unknown

Humor is to life what shock absorbers are to automobiles.

Unknown

A little nonsense, now and then, is relished by the wisest men.

Anonymous

He who laughs, lasts.

Mary Pettibone Poole

If you let your children think that Christians are always long-faced and sober, then you should not be surprised if they want nothing to do with Christianity. Christianity is the religion of joy, of singing and of gladness.

J. Vander Ploeg

One would be in less danger
From the wiles of the stranger
If one's own kin and kith
Were more fun to be with.

Ogden Nash

Be glad in the Lord. . .

Psalms 32:11, KJV

Good temper, like a sunny day, sheds a brightness over everything; it is the sweetener of toil and the soother of disquietude.

Washington Irving

Rejoice in the Lord always; and again I say, Rejoice.

Philippians 4:4, KJV

You have not fulfilled every duty, unless you have fulfilled that of being pleasant.

Charles Buxton

Have we talked with our children this week about the delights of living more than the disciplines of living? Have we inspired and guided them more than we have corrected them?

V. Gilbert Beers

The first duty to children is to make them happy. If you have not made them so, you have wronged them. No other good they may get can make up for that.

Charles Buxton

Fun times for great memories. . . so let's hear it for fewer frowns and more smiles. Laughter lingers. It soaks into the walls of a home, coming back to encourage us many years later.

Charles R. Swindoll

Providing
Good Examples

What this world needs is fewer rules and more good examples.

Unknown

Children are a great deal more apt to follow your lead than the way you point.

Unknown

There is just one way to bring up a child in the way he should go, and that is to travel that way yourself.

Abraham Lincoln

It is a great deal better to live a holy life than to talk about it.

Dwight L. Moody

Example is the school of mankind, and they will learn at no other.

Edmund Burke

Parents are patterns.

Thomas Fuller

Everywhere, we learn only from those whom we love.

Johann Wolfgang von Goethe

We are all of us more or less echoes, repeating involuntarily the virtues, the defects, the movements, and the characters of those among whom we live.

Joseph Joubert

Children miss nothing in sizing up their parents. . . Any ethical weak spot—any indecision on your part—will be incorporated and then magnified in your sons and daughters.

Dr. James Dobson

Thou shalt keep therefore his statutes, and his commandments. . . that it may go well with thee, and with thy children after thee. . .

Deuteronomy 4:40, KJV

Children pick up attitudes like a vacuum cleaner inhales dirt.

Howard G. Hendricks

The footsteps a boy follows are apt to be those his father thought he'd covered up.

Unknown

Children disgrace us in public by behaving just like we do at home.

Unknown

Of all commentaries upon the Scriptures, good examples are the best and the liveliest.

John Donne

Let your prayer be that God's goodness and the joy of Christ will shine through your life in such a way that your children will see the reality of your personal relationship with the Almighty God.

Dr. Kevin Leman

If you want to convince others of the value of Christianity—
live it!

Unknown

When a child watches you in the process of growth, watches Jesus Christ being formed in you, that is a highly com-
mendable thing to him.

Howard G. Hendricks

Let your light so shine before men, that they may see your
good works, and glorify your Father which is in heaven.

Matthew 5:16, KJV

The best way for a child to learn to fear God is to know a
real Christian. The best way for a child to
learn to pray is to live with
a father and mother
who know a life of
friendship with God,
and who truly pray.

Johann Heinrich
Pestalozzi

Every day, parents are in the process of teaching their children to honor or dishonor God, even if they never use religious words.

Gary Smalley and John Trent, Ph.D.

Training must start within the parent. Nothing can really happen *through* us until it has happened to us. Children will have a great respect for instruction if they witness a genuineness in the models of their moms and dads.

Charles R. Swindoll

Do your kids see you taking time out to read the Bible? Do they see you allowing the Word of God to seep into your life and behavior? Do your kids see you trusting God even when things go wrong? Growing up is never easy and what your kids see in your life is often more important than what they hear.

Tim Hansel

The serene beauty of a holy life is the most powerful influence in the world next to the power of God.

Blaise Pascal

There is no such reward for a well-spent life as to see one's children well started in life, owing to their parents' good health, good principles, fixed character, good breeding, and in general the whole outfit, that enables them to fight the battle of life with success.

William Graham Sumner

No good action, no good example dies. It lives forever in our race. While the frame molders and disappears, the deed leaves an indelible stamp, and moulds the very thought and will of future generations.

Samuel Smiles

Goodness is the only investment that never fails.

Henry David Thoreau

There is not a man or woman, however poor they may be, but have it in their power, by the grace of God, to leave behind them the grandest thing on earth, character; and their children might rise up after them and thank God that their mother was a pious woman, or their father a pious man.

Norman McLeod

Passing on Faith

Kids today learn a lot about getting to the moon, but very little about getting to Heaven.

David Jeremiah

Many parents do nothing about their children's religious education, telling them they can decide what they believe when they're twenty-one. That's like telling them they can decide when they're twenty-one, whether or not they should brush their teeth. By then, their teeth may have fallen out. Likewise, their principles and morality may also be non-existent.

Princess Grace of Monaco

Time is so fleeting that if we do not remember God in our youth, age may find us incapable of thinking about Him.

Hans Christian Anderson

A house without a roof would scarcely be a more different home, than a family unsheltered by God's friendship, and the sense of being always rested in His providential care and guidance.

Horace Bushnell

When parents say they are going to withhold indoctrination from their small child, allowing him to "decide for himself," they are almost guaranteeing that he will "decide" in the negative.

Dr. James Dobson

We are the guardians of our children's souls, and there is no need to feel helpless, or to apologize to anyone, in deciding to raise our children in the love and admonition of God.

Clifford Stunden

For parents to see a child growing up without Christ is a far greater dereliction of duty than for parents to have children who grow up without learning to read or write.

Donald Grey Barnhouse

A man is shaped to beliefs long held however uncritically— as the roots of a tree that has grown in the crevices of a rock.

Justice Oliver Wendell Holmes, Jr.

So great is my veneration for the Bible that the earlier my children begin to read it, the more confident will be my hope that they will prove useful citizens to their country, and respectable members of society.

John Quincy Adams

As for me and my house, we will serve the Lord.

Joshua 24:15, KJV

I prayed for this child, and the Lord has granted me what I asked of him. So now I give him to the Lord. . .

I Samuel 1:27-28, NIV

Only take heed to thyself, and keep thy soul diligently, lest thou forget the things which thine eyes have seen, and lest they depart from thy heart all the days of thy life: but teach them thy sons, and thy sons' sons. . .

Deuteronomy 4:9, KJV

"Go home to your family and tell them how much the Lord has done for you, and how he has had mercy on you."

Mark 5:19, NIV

Thank God for pastors, Sunday school teachers, club leaders, and all the rest—but their efforts are not enough. No matter how much they talk, the child still sits and mulls a silent question: *I wonder what my folks think of all this?*

Dean and Grace Merrill

Tell ye your children of it (the Word of the Lord), and let your children tell their children, and their children another generation.

Joel 1:3, KJV

The family circle is the supreme conductor of Christianity.

Henry Drummond

If you want your (child) to know what Christ will do for him, let him see what Christ has done for you.

Unknown

People are guided to heaven more by footprints than by guideposts.

Unknown

And I pray that as you share your faith with others it will grip their lives too, as they see the wealth of good things in you that come from Christ Jesus.

Philemon 6, TLB

Parents who want their children to know God must culti-vate their own relationship with God. . . How can we con-vince our children that God is important, if we never give Him any of our time? How can we pretend to love Him, when we scarcely spend a minute with Him alone?

Larry Christenson

He who has no fire in himself cannot warm others.

Unknown

The time is past when parents can give their children a pleasant surface-coating of religion. Our children are either going to be filled with Jesus and excited about Him, or filled with sin and excited about it. All that we can bring our chil-dren will be worthless unless we can bring them Jesus.

Larry Christenson

If we hope to instill within (our chil-dren) a faith that will last a life-time, then they must see and feel our passion for God.

Dr. James Dobson

No one can give faith unless he has faith. It is the persuaded who persuade.

Joseph Joubert

Young people today are looking for involvement. If we as parents have a soft religion, we're not going to offer any challenge.

Adrian Rogers

References to spiritual things are not to be reserved just for Sunday morning or even for bedtime prayer. They should permeate our conversation and the fabric of our lives.

Dr. James Dobson

The family was ordained of God that children might be trained up for himself; it was before the church, or rather the first form of the church on earth.

Pope Leo XIII

I have now disposed of all my property to my family. There is one thing more I wish I could give them, and that is the Christian religion. If they had that, and I had not given them one shilling, they would have been rich, and if they had not that, and I had given them all the world, they would be poor.

Patrick Henry

Loving Unconditionally

Love isn't scared.
it builds bridges instead of walls.
it never gives up.
it always hangs on.
it waits with stubborn, strong hope.
sometimes even years.

Ann Kiemel

Love keeps giving when tired, or busy, or sick, or bored—
or what have you.

Howard G. Hendricks

Love is patient, love is kind. It does not envy, it does not boast, it is not proud. It is not rude, it is not self-seeking, it is not easily angered, it keeps no record of wrongs. Love does not delight in evil but rejoices with the truth. It always protects, always trusts, always hopes, always perseveres. Love never fails.

I Corinthians 13:4-8, NIV

Love can hope where reason would despair.

George Baron Lyttelton

Love feels no burdens, thinks nothing of trouble, attempts what is above its strength, pleads no excuse of impossibility. It is therefore able to undertake all things, and it completes many things, and warrants them to take effect, where he who does not love would faint and lie down.

Thomas a' Kempis

Faith—makes all things possible.
Hope—makes all things bright.
But love—makes all things easy.

Unknown

Jacob served seven years for Rachel; and they seemed unto him *but* a few days, for the love he had to her.

Genesis 29:20, KJV

If we spend our lives in loving, we have no leisure to complain, or to feel unhappiness.

Joseph Joubert

Love never reasons, but profusely gives; gives, like a thoughtless prodigal, its all, and trembles then lest it has done too little.

Hannah More

I believe that love—steady, patient, unceasing, deep, expressed, oozed—is the only reliable option open to parents. It's better than advice, grounding, cutting the allowance, paddlings, punishments and threats or any of the dozens of dodges and ruses we work on our unsuspecting and waiting children. Just care, just love, just show it.

Margaret F. Skutch

Remember, there is a time for love and a place for love. Anytime, any place.

Bruce and Cheryl Bickel,
Stan and Karin Jantz

Where love is, there's no lack.

Richard Brome

Love each other deeply, because love covers over a multitude of sins.

I Peter 4:8, NIV

Parents who expect obedience but neglect to balance that with an equal amount of supporting love run a substantial risk of having their children lured into an element of society that will give them that love. . . Frankly, our children are not really going to care how much we know until they know how much we care.

Clifford Stunden

Force may subdue, but love gains, and he who forgives first wins the laurel.

William Penn

A pennyweight o' love is worth a pound o' law.

Old Proverb

Men are won, not so much by being blamed, as by being encompassed with love.
William Ellery Channing

A child's most important reason for wanting to be good is the love of his parents for him. When that is lost he has little motivation to be good.
John M. Drescher

Love and a cough cannot be hid.

George Herbert

Moments of quiet, complete attention do more to communicate our love than almost any other single thing. They also do more to prevent family problems and conflicts than anything I know!

Dr. Bruce Narramore

Love always acts in the child's best interests, even if the child does not understand at that particular point in time. You are not interested in how he feels and reacts now as much as how he feels and reacts 10 to 15 years from now. True love treats the child now in terms of the future.

Howard G. Hendricks

When a family goes through a period of rebellion with a child, it is important to say, "There's not anything you can do to make us stop loving you."

David Jeremiah

Love is to be a way of life, woven into the fabric of living. Not a glossy finish that cracks when it's best, but a dyed-in-the-wool hue that pervades the whole home. How do children catch this? Like chicken pox—from exposure.

Howard G. Hendricks

We can make a child feel his immense worth by showing him our unconditional love. This means we accept our children fully, no matter how they act. When children disobey, we discipline, but we shouldn't attack their character. . . We should focus on the misdeed, not on our children's sense of worth.

Dr. Bruce Narramore

Be completely humble and gentle; be patient, bearing with one another in love.

Ephesians 4:2, NIV

The greatest happiness of life is the conviction that we are loved—loved for ourselves, or rather, loved in spite of ourselves.

Victor Hugo

Our first goal in moral training must be to help our children develop their ability to love. This ability comes only as children first experience love from us. . . Before we ask our children to do loving things for other people, they must feel strongly loved themselves.

Dr. Bruce Narramore

Give a little love to a child, and you get a great deal back.

John Ruskin

Freely ye have received, freely give.

Matthew 10:8, KJV

And the Lord make you to increase and abound in love one toward another.

I Thessalonian 3:12, KJV

Praising Generously

If a child lives with praise, he learns to appreciate. An adult can get along without daily praise. A child cannot. He must have it to develop. He will shrivel up without praise.

John M. Drescher

A child is fed with milk and praise.

Mary Lamb

A child's happy awareness that he or she is valuable is maintained through consistent, sincere praise.

Paul Lewis

Pleasant words are as an honeycomb, sweet to the soul, and health to the bones.

Proverbs 16:24, KJV

A word spoken in due season, how good is it!

Proverbs 15:23, KJV

Raise a child's self-esteem by playing the game of "Caught ya!" The idea is to catch the child being good, and to comment on whatever it is the child is doing.

Linda Albert

Good words are worth much, and cost little.

George Herbert

Kind words are the bright flowers of earthly existence; use them, and especially around the fireside circle. They are jewels beyond price, and powerful to heal the wounded heart and make the weighed-down spirit glad.

Arthur Helps

One thing scientists have discovered is that often-praised children become more intelligent than often-blamed ones. There's a creative element in praise.

Thomas Dreier

Most parents attack what their children do wrong much more often than they affirm what their children do right.

Dr. Kenneth Story

I praise loudly; I blame softly.

Catherine II of Russia

Good words do more than hard speeches, as the sunbeams, without any noise, will make the traveler cast off his cloak, which all the blustering winds could not do, but only make him bind it closer to him.

Robert Leighton

Reprove thy (child) privately; commend him publicly.

Solon

A child's behavior is linked to his self-esteem.
Praise encourages good behavior and good self-esteem.

Freda Ingle Briggs

The surest way to knock the chip off a fellow's shoulder is by patting him on the back.

Zig Ziglar

Words of praise, indeed, are almost as necessary to warm a child into a congenial life as acts of kindness and affection. Judicious praise is to children what the sun is to flowers.

Christian Nestell Bovee

Praise is a power for good; both God and man prize it. . . The best worker, if his fellows fail to praise, fails to do as well as he can.

Anonymous

All of us, in the glow of feeling we have pleased, want to do more to please. When we are told we have done well, we want to do better. Dr. George W. Crane, author and social psychologist, said, "The art of praising is the beginning of the fine art of pleasing."

John M. Drescher

Nearly every one of us is starving to be appreciated, and when someone comes along who genuinely thanks us, we will follow that person a very long way.

Alan Loy McGinnis

Kind words produce their own image in men's souls; and a beautiful image it is. They soothe and quiet and comfort the hearer. They shame him out of his sour, morose, unkind feelings. We have not yet begun to use kind words in such abundance as they ought to be used.

Blaise Pascal

Verbal reinforcement can be the strongest motivator of human behavior.

Dr. James Dobson

The applause of a single human being is of great consequence.

Samuel Johnson

Therefore encourage one another and build each other up, just as in fact you are doing.

I Thessalonians 5:11, NIV

In praising or loving a child, we love and praise not that which is, but that which we hope for.

Johann Wolfgang von Goethe

Your child is wet cement, and affirmations are the forms to mold his future shape.

Anne Ortlund

Praying Without Stopping

Pray! Yes, pray. It is one of those disciplines we do too little of as it relates to our family relationships.

Charles R. Swindoll

Pray without ceasing.

I Thessalonians 5:17, KJV

And pray in the Spirit on all occasions with all kinds of prayers and requests.

Ephesians 6:18, NIV

Do not be anxious about anything, but in everything, by prayer and petition, with thanksgiving, present your requests to God.

Philippians 4:6, NIV

We must bathe (our children) in prayer every day of their lives. The God who made your children will hear your petitions. He has promised to do so. After all, He loves them more than you do.

Dr. James Dobson

Prayer is to a family what a roof is to a house; it protects those within from the enemies and adversities of life.

Unknown

I know of no blessing so small as to be reasonably expected without prayer, nor any so great but may be attained by it.

Robert South

If Christians spent as much time praying as they do grumbling, they would have nothing to grumble about.

Anonymous

Trouble and perplexity drive me to prayer, and prayer drives away perplexity and trouble.

Philip Melanchthon

Let us therefore come boldly unto the throne of grace, that we may obtain mercy, and find grace to help in time of need.

Hebrews 4:16, KJV

I have been driven many times to my knees by the over-whelming conviction that I had nowhere else to go.

Abraham Lincoln

In the day of my trouble I will call upon thee: for thou wilt answer me.

Psalms 86:7, KJV

O, do not pray for easy lives. Pray to be stronger men. Do not pray for tasks equal to your powers. Pray for powers equal to your tasks.

Phillips Brooks

No prayer, no power; little prayer, little power. Much prayer, much power.

Peter Deyneka

If ye abide in me, and my words abide in you, ye shall ask what ye will, and it shall be done unto you.

John 15:7, KJV

Like a marksman with a rusty rifle, like an archer with an

unstrung bow is the parent. . . with a slipshod prayer life. He who has little intimacy with God will secure few blessings for his family.

Larry Christenson

Those who run from God in the morning will scarcely find him the rest of the day.

John Bunyan

We must feed on the Bread of Life ourselves before we can serve it to others.

Unknown

Is prayer your steering wheel or your spare tire?

Corrie ten Boom

Prayers can't be answered unless they are prayed.

Unknown

Don't pray when you feel like it. Have an appointment with the Lord and keep it. A man is powerful on his knees.

Corrie ten Boom

If you don't set a definite time for prayer, just like a definite time to go to work, watch a ball game or meet an appointment at the dentist, you just won't pray.

Ron Rand

Forbidding prayers in school won't hurt our country half as much as forgetting prayers at home.

Unknown

Where two or three are gathered in my name, there am I in the midst of them.

Matthew 18:20, KJV

The family that prays together stays together.

American Proverb

I consider praying for my children to be the most significant thing I do for them. . . I reversed this process, too, asking my children to pray for me. I admitted my needs to my children, even when they were young.

Evelyn Christenson

Confess your faults one to another, and pray one for another.

James 5:16, KJV

All the duties of religion are eminently solemn and venerable in the eyes of children. But none will so strongly prove the sincerity of the parent; none so powerfully awake the reverence of the child; none so happily recommend the instruction he receives, as family devotions, particularly those in which petitions for the children occupy a distinguished place.

John S. Dwight

Make sure your family prayers begin with praise and thanksgiving before you make requests.

Paul Lewis

He who has learned how to pray has learned the greatest secret of a holy and happy life.

William Law

Early in our own family life, we used a loose-leaf notebook. On one side was written, "We Ask," and on the other side, "He Answers." I wouldn't exchange for anything what this taught my children about the theology of prayer.

Howard G. Hendricks

More things are wrought by prayer
Than this world dreams of. . .

Alfred, Lord Tennyson

Urge your child to pray and ask God's forgiveness and explain that spankings don't remove or forgive sin, only Jesus can do that.

David Jeremiah

Prayer is a powerful thing, for God has bound and tied himself thereto. None can believe how powerful prayer is, and what it is able to effect, but those who have learned it by experience.

Martin Luther

The lost art in prayer is that of listening. . . Parenting is at its best when you cultivate the art of listening to your true self, to your children's real needs, and most of all to God and His agenda for all of you.

Dr. Emil Authelet

And I say unto you, ask, and it shall be given you; seek, and ye shall find; knock, and it shall be opened unto you. every one that asketh receiveth; and he that seeketh findeth; and to him that knocketh it shall be opened.

Luke 11:9-10, KJV

Teaching Responsibility

You are not responsible for how your children behave; they are. If you try to assume responsibility for their actions, it will make both of you angry. Your only responsibility is to make sure that your children are rewarded when they behave properly and suffer the consequences when they misbehave.

Patrick J. Jeske

I believe the Christian home should be a place where children can learn to make decisions about their lives and learn to accept the consequences of their decisions—the good and the bad.

Dr. Kevin Leman

I'm trying to realize that I must allow my children to accept their own problems. I can't go around constantly fixing problems for them. Instead, I want to give them the skills and attitudes they need to learn to solve problems on their own.

Tim Hansel

Responsibility educates.

Wendell Phillips

Feeling a real part of the family does not just happen—you create it in (your child) through having him share the responsibilities. How well he can do the task, though, is not important. This will improve through practice. What is important is that he feels capable.

Dr. Emil Authelet

Our objective as parents. . . is to do nothing for boys and girls which they can profit from doing for themselves.

Dr. James Dobson

Ability involves responsibility.

Alexander MacLaren

Few things help an individual more than to place responsibility upon him, and to let him know that you trust him.

Booker T. Washington

It is good for children to see the connection between responsible behavior and privilege. As they learn to be responsible in their actions, they should be given more privileges. This type of trust builds maturity.

Jay Kesler

The price of greatness is responsibility.

Winston Churchill

The greatest ABILITY is DEPENDABILITY.

Unknown

He that is faithful in that which is least is faithful also in much.

Luke 16:10, KJV

Each year, more responsibility and freedom (they are companions) are given to the child so that the final release in early adulthood is merely the final relaxation of authority.

Dr. James Dobson

Responsibility walks hand in hand with capacity and power.

Josiah Gilbert Holland

Action springs not from thought, but from a readiness for responsibility.

Dietrich Bonhoeffer

Remember, your basic assignment as a parent is to work yourself out of a job.

Paul Lewis

Taking Time Together

Can he be a good Christian that spends all his religion abroad and leaves none for his nearest relations at home?

William Gurnall

If the dishes wait, we see the problem immediately. If the lawn waits, we notice the results in a week or two. But when a child waits, we may not see the result for years. Then we look back and wonder, "Where did I go wrong?"

Dr. Bruce Narramore

It is difficult to be a good parent. There are no magic potions or formulas. One of the great myths in our society is that we can be parents without real investment of time and energy.

Tim Hansel

God travels at a snail's pace. Those who want to do good are not selfish, they are not in a hurry, they know that to impregnate people with good requires a long time.

Mahatma Gandhi

The best thing to spend on children is your time.

Unknown

Games are outgrown and toys decay,
But he'll never forget if you give him a day.

Unknown

Let me suggest a family night at least once a week. (With no television, okay?). . . The kids will grow to love it, believe me. And God will give you all kinds of insight into each child during those special evenings together.

Charles R. Swindoll

Moments of uninhibited communication between child and parent cannot be planned; they just happen. The only ingredient we bring to that dynamic of family life is our availability. . . and that is spelled T-I-M-E.

David Jeremiah

Let's start saying no to more and more of the things that pull us farther and farther away from the ones who need us the most. Let's remember that the greatest earthly gifts we can provide are our presence and influence while we live and a magnificent memory of our lives once we're gone.

Charles R. Swindoll

Any time you spend, working, playing, or loafing, with your children makes them feel more worthwhile than any A+ can.

Sara D. Gilbert

The time and energy investment bargain of all time is that time and effort you give to your kids. Dividends will come your way all your life.

Zig Ziglar

Breathes there a kid who doesn't enjoy playing a game with his parents? And breathes there a parent past fifty who doesn't regret taking so little time for games when the kids were young?

Dean and Grace Merrill

It is best to be with those in time, that we hope to be with in eternity.

Thomas Fuller

As we have therefore opportunity, let us do good unto all men, especially unto them who are of the household of faith.

Galatians 6:10, KJV

There will always be worthwhile causes, but not always a two-year-old in your lap.

Freda Ingle Briggs

Alas! how swift the moments fly!
How flash the years along!

John Quincy Adams

Each day you have a child in your home is a day you capture or lose in preparing him to go.

Gary Smalley and John Trent, Ph.D.

My days are swifter than a weaver's shuttle.

Job 7:6, KJV

You may delay, but time will not.

Benjamin Franklin

As every thread of gold is valuable, so is every moment of time.

John Mason

There is not a single moment in life that we can afford to lose.

Edward M. Goulburn

Bless our home, Father,
That we may cherish the bread before there is none,
Discover each other before we leave,
And enjoy each other for what we are while we have time.

Prayer on a sampler

Acknowledgments

The editor and the publisher have made every effort to trace the ownership of all copyrighted material and to secure permission from copyright holders of such material. In the event of any question arising as to the use of any material, the publisher and editor, while expressing regret for inadvertent error, will be pleased to make the necessary corrections in future printings. Thanks are due to the following authors, publishers, publications and agents for permission to use the material indicated.

ANN KIEMEL ANDERSON: *I Love The Word Impossible* by Ann Kiemel. Copyright 1978 by Tyndale House Publishers.

AUGSBURG FORTRESS PUBLISHERS: *Bible Readings* by Mildred Tengbom. Copyright 1987 by Augsburg Publishing House. *Bringing Out The Best In People* by Alan Loy McGinnis. Copyright 1985 by Augsburg Publishing House. Both used by permission of Augsburg Fortress.

BAKER BOOK HOUSE COMPANY: *Devotions For Mothers* compiled by Hester M. Monsma. Copyright 1984 by Baker Book House Company.

BARBOUR AND COMPANY, INC: *Life's Little Handbook Of Wisdom* by Bruce and Cheryl Bickel and Stan and Karin Jantz. Copyright 1992 by Barbour and Company, Inc.

V. GILBERT BEERS: "William Bloomer's Footprints" by V. Gilbert Beers. *Christianity Today*, June 12, 1987.

BETHANY HOUSE PUBLISHERS: *The Christian Family* by Larry Christenson. Copyright 1970 by Bethany House Publishers, Minneapolis, MN.

FREDA A. BRIGGS: *Mom, Can We Still Keep Roger?* by Freda Ingle Briggs. Copyright 1985 by Baker Book House.

DONALD J. CARTER: *String Of Pearls* by Mary C. Crowley. Copyright 1985 by Word Books.